GREAT ⊕ CIVILISATIONS

INDUS VALLEY

Anita Ganeri

First published in 2014 by Franklin Watts

Copyright © Franklin Watts 2014

Franklin Watts
338 Euston Road
London NW1 3BH

Franklin Watts Australia
Level 17/207 Kent Street
Sydney, NSW 2000

A CIP catalogue record for the book is available from the British Library.

Dewey number: 934

Hardback ISBN 978 1 4451 3396 6
Library eBook ISBN 978 1 4451 3397 3

Printed in China

Franklin Watts is a division of Hachette Children's Books,
an Hachette UK company.

www.hachette.co.uk

Editor: Sarah Ridley
Editor in Chief: John C. Miles
Series designer: John Christopher/White Design
Art director: Peter Scoulding
Picture research: Kathy Lockley

CONTENTS

THE INDUS VALLEY

About five thousand years ago, a great civilisation grew up around the Indus River in modern-day Pakistan and north-west India. At its peak, around 2600-1900 BCE, the Indus Valley Civilisation covered more land area than ancient Egypt. It had busy cities, such as Harappa and Mohenjo-Daro, thriving trade links, skilled craftspeople and superb engineers.

4

Remains

We know about the Indus Valley Civilisation from the city ruins, jewellery, pots and clay figures that were left behind. Archaeologists have also found hundreds of small, square stone seals (see page 19), carved with pictures of people and animals. The seals have symbols that look like writing but, so far, no one has been able to work out what the writing says.

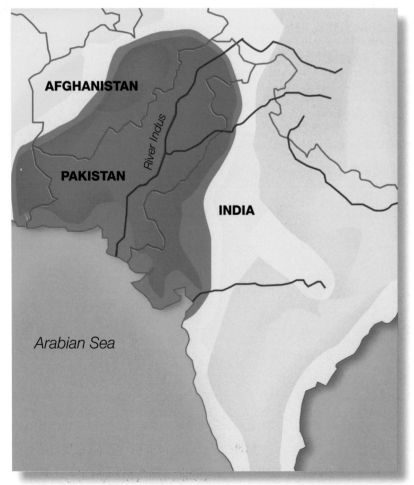

Land of the Indus

The Indus River begins in the Himalaya mountains, then flows almost 3,000 kilometres to the Arabian Sea. It was the lifeblood of the Indus Valley Civilisation. Farmers relied on the annual flooding of the river to grow crops, such as wheat, barley and melons. The river was also vital for trade. Further Indus sites have been found along the coast, and along the dried-up river beds of the Ghaggar-Hakra river.

This map shows the location and extent of the Indus Valley Civilisation in green. Modern borders are shown in red, rivers in blue.

Discovering the Indus

After its collapse around 1900 BCE, the Indus Valley Civilisation disappeared. Then, in 1826, British traveller, Charles Masson, noticed a mysterious brick mound which he thought looked like a ruined castle. In fact, he had stumbled on the long-lost city of Harappa. Later, many of the bricks were removed to build a railway, but in the 1920s, archaeologists began to excavate Harappa and Mohenjo-Daro properly. They found the remains of two enormous cities, thousands of years old.

The ruins of Mohenjo-Daro were discovered in 1922. It was one of the biggest cities of the Indus Valley Civilisation.

5

Dating the Indus Valley

We do not have exact dates for the artefacts found at the Indus sites. Using various techniques, however, archaeologists have been able to place the civilisation between the years 2600–1700 BCE. One technique is called radiocarbon dating. All living things contain the element carbon 14 which decays at a known rate. Experts can use this to work out the age of objects made from materials such as bone, wood and shell.

 ## Around the world

c. 4000–2000 BCE Sumeria
One of the earliest civilisations grows up in Sumer (modern-day Iraq) on the fertile land around the great Tigris and Euphrates rivers.

c. 3000–30 BCE Egypt
The ancient Egyptians build one of the world's earliest, greatest and longest-lasting civilisations along the banks of the River Nile.

c. 1600–1460 BCE China
The Shang Dynasty rules in the Yellow River valley region of China. Their capital moves several times, finally to a place called Anyang.

SCULPTOR'S SKILLS

Even though the Indus Valley people left no paintings or large-scale sculptures, we know that their craftspeople were highly skilled. Every Indus city had workshops where potters, metal-workers, stone-workers and seal-makers (see page 19) produced high quality goods for use at home and for trading abroad.

6

Dancing girl

This little figure found at Mohenjo-Daro is one of the most famous Indus artefacts. Known as the 'dancing girl', it stands 10.5 cm high and is made from bronze. The girl's hair is tied in a plait and she is wearing bangles on her arms. The statue is not only a sign of the skill of the Indus person who made it, but also gives us a glimpse into Indus life. It shows that dance was probably an important form of entertainment in Indus times.

Cutting edge

Several different types of potters' kilns have been excavated (uncovered), showing that Indus potters used a wide range of techniques. A double-chambered kiln contained a lower chamber for fuel and a separate upper chamber where pots were placed to be fired. This made it easier for the potter to control the temperature of the kiln.

The famous Indus dancing girl statuette from Mohenjo-Daro dates from around 2500 BCE.

This kiln at Mohenjo-Daro was used to fire pots and other small clay objects.

Pottery pieces

Many pots and pieces of pottery have been found at Indus sites. More than 100 different types of pot have been identified. They were used for storing food, water and wine at home, and for transporting goods, often over long distances. Indus pots have been found as far away as Saudi Arabia. Pots were also placed in people's graves (see pages 26-27). Most Indus pots are plain but some were decorated in red and black.

 ## Around the world

c. 6000–4000 BCE Mesopotamia
The potter's wheel is invented in Mesopotamia. A stone wheel from the city of Ur dates from around 3129 BCE but wheels were also used in Egypt and the Indus Valley.

c. 3000 BCE Egypt
The Egyptians become experts at making a glassy blue-green material, called faience, by grinding quartz or sand crystals with other minerals.

c. 1600–1460 BCE China
Bronze casting advances during the Shang Dynasty. Bronze is mainly used for making weapons, as well as objects for ceremonies.

BEADS AND BANGLES

Archaeologists have found evidence that people – both men and women – in the Indus Valley wore jewellery, especially bead necklaces, bangles, brooches and earrings. They were made by highly skilled craftspeople, using materials such as gold, copper, sea shells, clay and semi-precious stones, such as agate, lapis lazuli, jasper and carnelian.

Cutting edge

We do not know for certain what Indus Valley people wore because no remains of clothing have been found. However, we do know that Indus farmers grew cotton and kept sheep, so it seems likely that clothes were woven from cotton, which was cooler in summer, and wool, which was warmer in winter.

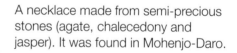

A necklace made from semi-precious stones (agate, chalecedony and jasper). It was found in Mohenjo-Daro.

Bead-makers

Remains of beads, bead-making tools and bead-makers' workshops have been found in many Indus sites. To make beads from carnelian, the person chipped away at the stone until it was the right size and shape. A hole was cut in each bead, using a small stone drill. Finally, the beads were polished with a mixture of water and sand-like powder, and heated in a kiln until they turned dark red. This colour was highly valued by wealthy Indus citizens and traders.

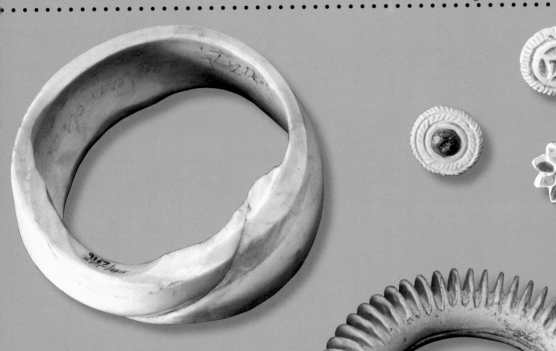

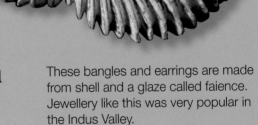

9

Wearing bangles

Women and men in the Indus Valley wore bangles made from shell, clay and copper. Shell bangles were made in towns close to the sea, such as Balakot. In one workshop, the bangles were made from clam shells; in the other, from conch shells. Stoneware bangles were made from clay on a potter's wheel and then fired inside large jars.

These bangles and earrings are made from shell and a glaze called faience. Jewellery like this was very popular in the Indus Valley.

Around the world

c. 5000 BCE Egypt

One of the earliest examples of woven cloth comes from the city of Fayum in Egypt. Strips of linen have also been found in Egyptian tombs. They were used to wrap mummies.

c. 2600–2000 BCE Sumeria

Huge quantities of gold and silver jewellery are buried in the Royal Tombs of Ur, including an extraordinary headdress of gold leaves and gold ribbons, worn by Queen Puabi.

c. 2000 BCE–900 CE Central America

The Maya make exquisite jewellery from jade, including earplugs, worn by the men. Jade is also traded, used by healers to cure the sick, and offered to the gods.

FARMING FOR FOOD

The fertile floodplains around the River Indus provided farmers with the ideal place to grow crops. This meant that they were able to supply enough food to feed the large numbers of people in the Indus cities. By examining skeletons and the contents of rubbish pits, archaeologists think that Indus people generally ate a healthy diet, with grains, fruit, vegetables, meat and milk.

10

Cutting edge

Artefacts from the city of Mehrgarh give us clues about how Indus people prepared and cooked their food. At first, food was cooked by 'stone boiling'. Stones were heated in the fire, then placed in tar-lined baskets containing liquid and food. The tar stopped the basket from leaking. Later, clay cooking pots were used instead and heated on the fire.

Seasonal crops

Indus farmers grew grains, such as wheat, barley, millet, and peas, lentils and chickpeas. Grains were used to make bread and porridge, and fermented to make beer and wine. Peas, lentils and chickpeas were dried and stored. Farmers also grew fruits, such as melons, grapes and dates, and raised cattle, sheep and goats. Different crops were planted for winter (which was wet and mild) and summer (which was hot and dry).

This small clay model of a cart pulled by bullocks shows that Indus farmers transported grain or other harvested crops in large clay pots.

Grain store mystery

The Great Granary at Harappa is a huge building more than 45 metres long. It has two rows of six large rooms, arranged along a central passageway. A wooden roof, supported by large columns, would have been built over the top. At first, archaeologists thought that this was a huge granary (grain store) but there is no sign of any grain or storage containers. It may have been a palace or a meeting place for the city's leaders but no one knows for sure.

11

The Great Granary at Harappa is an impressive building, but nobody really knows if it's a granary or not. This photograph shows a long passageway that runs down the middle of the site.

Around the world

c. 4000 BCE Sumeria
The Sumerians have well-organised farms, growing barley, wheat, dates, apples and plums. They use ploughs pulled by oxen to plough their fields.

c. 2000 BCE Egypt
The Egyptians invent the shaduf, a device that helps farmers to draw water from the river and use it to irrigate their fields. Shadufs are still in use today.

c. 2000 BCE–900 CE Central America
Maize is such an important crop for the Mayan civilisation that they worship several maize gods, and believe that their ancestors were made from maize.

CITIES AND SOCIETY

The ruins of hundreds of large and well-organised cities have been found in the Indus Valley. They were the first cities in the region and marked a remarkable shift in how people lived. The biggest cities were Mohenjo-Daro and Harappa, with populations of 30–40,000 people each.

12 City planning

The remarkable thing about the Indus cities was how well-planned they were. They were laid out on a strict grid system, with straight roads crossing each other. Main streets were up to ten metres wide, large enough for carts to pass. Some cities, such as Mohenjo-Daro, had a citadel, built on top of a mound. This may have been used for religious ceremonies or public meetings. Most people lived in the lower part of the city.

Cutting edge
Archaeologists continue to work at Mohenjo-Daro but are no longer allowed to do any digging in case they damage the buildings. Instead, they have been using instruments, such as cameras attached to unmanned hot-air balloons to take aerial photographs, and specially designed vacuum cleaners to blow away loose layers of dust and debris.

The citadel at Mohenjo-Daro, with the lower town in the foreground and the walls of houses where people lived.

Priest-King?

We do not know who was in charge of the Indus cities. There is no evidence for any leaders or kings. This 17-cm-high stone statue was found in Mohenjo-Daro in 1927 and shows the head of an important-looking man with a beard and headband. He is wearing an elaborate robe with a three-leaf pattern on it. Archaeologists named the statue the 'Priest-King' but we do not know if he was a priest or a king, or neither.

13

The famous head of the 'Priest-King' dates from between 2200 and 1900 BCE. The carved leaf shapes were originally painted red.

 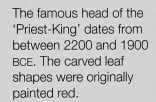

Around the world

c. 3800 BCE Sumeria
The Sumerian cities of Ur, Uruk and Eridu are among the earliest cities. Some experts argue that Eridu is the oldest city in the world.

c. 331 BCE Egypt
Alexander the Great founds the city of Alexandria. It grew to become the largest city in the ancient world and a famous centre of learning.

c. 2000 BCE–900 CE Central America
The Maya build great cities, such as Tikal, Chichen Itza and Palenque, each ruled by its own powerful king.

DAILY LIFE

Apart from large public buildings, archaeologists have also found the ruins of hundreds of workshops, storage units and homes in the Indus cities, like the ones shown below at Mohenjo-Daro.
The buildings are made from mud bricks, baked hard in a kiln. Houses were crowded together and were divided from each other by walls.

Cutting edge

The bricks used to build the Indus cities were so strong that they have lasted for thousands of years. They were made from a mixture of clay, soil and water, pressed into a brick-shaped wooden mould. The bricks were baked in the sun or put inside a kiln to fire them. They were usually made in two sizes – smaller for houses, and larger for walls and platforms.

Leisure time

Among the artefacts found in Indus houses are many children's toys, such as toy animals and toy carts, made from baked clay. Indus people also seemed to like playing board games. At Harappa, archaeologists have found dice made from cubes of clay and sandstone. They have six sides, with one to six spots. These may be the oldest dice in the world.

15

This solid stone board and carved pieces seem to have been used to play a game that was like chess. Players moved from square to square.

Inside an Indus house

A typical house in Mohenjo-Daro was two or three storeys tall with the different rooms arranged around a central courtyard. Houses had thick walls to keep them cool, and there were no windows onto the main street in order to keep out dust and noise. They also had flat roofs which families could use as an extra room. Sometimes, the entrance to the house was through the roof.

The walls of Indus houses were made from fired mud bricks, making them strong and long-lasting.

 ## Around the world

c. 7500 BCE Middle East
The oldest known bricks, made from mud, are found at Tell Aswad in Syria. Ancient bricks have also been found in southern Turkey and around Jericho in the West Bank.

c. 3300 BCE Egypt
Senet, one of the world's oldest board games, is played in ancient Egypt. A senet board is buried in the tomb of Tutankhamun.

206 BCE–220 CE China
During the Han Dynasty, miniature clay models of houses and other buildings are often placed in a dead person's grave.

CLEAN WATER

The Indus Valley people invented sophisticated ways of bringing clean water to their cities, and taking away dirty water and sewage. Their sanitation system was a great feat of engineering, which no other ancient civilisation came close to matching.

Water supply

16

In the cities, most people fetched water for washing and drinking from public wells dug in the streets. A few houses had their own private wells. The main streets were also lined with brick drains. Waste water and sewage from houses flowed along the drains into cesspits, located well away from where people lived and worked. Stairs led down into the cesspits to allow cleaners to dig out the pits and take the waste away.

Cutting edge

Indus houses were the first in the world to have bathrooms and toilets. Toilets were built from bricks with brick or wooden seats. The waste flowed through pipes in the wall into a drain in the street. To wash, people stood on a brick 'shower tray' and poured water over themselves from a jar. Again, the dirty water flowed out into a drain.

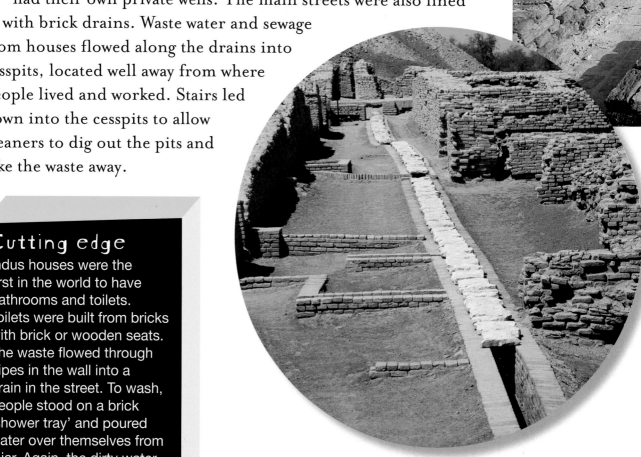

A brick drain running along a street in Mohenjo-Daro. It carried waste water to collecting tanks and eventually to the countryside.

Priests may have washed in the Great Bath to purify themselves before religious ceremonies.

The Great Bath

The Great Bath in Mohenjo-Daro looks like a large swimming pool. It was 12 metres long, 2.4 metres deep, and was built of bricks, joined together with tar so that the water did not leak out. Stairs at either end led down into the bath. Around the bath was a courtyard, leading to small rooms and a well that supplied the water. No one is sure what the Great Bath was used for. It may have been a public bath or have been used for religious ceremonies.

Around the world

c. 2600–1900 BCE Asia
Many of the houses in Indus cities are raised up on huge brick platforms to stop them being flooded when the river bursts its banks.

c. 1900 BCE Greece
The Minoan city of Knossos on Crete has an advanced sanitation system and an example of one of the world's first flushing toilets.

c. 600 BCE Italy
The Romans build the *Cloaca Maxima*, one of the world's earliest sewage systems. It drains waste from the city of Rome into the River Tiber.

TRADING PARTNERS

Trade was extremely important to the Indus Valley Civilisation. Among the goods traded were beads, bangles and pots, in exchange for materials, such as metals and semi-precious stones. Traders travelled long distances – to Afghanistan, Arabia and Mesopotamia – by foot, bullock cart and boat (see pages 20-21). Indus seals have been found in Mesopotamia.

18

Trade goods

In several Indus cities, archaeologists have found pots filled with valuable objects, such as metal tools and weapons, jewellery and semi-precious stones. These were found under floors and near blocked-up doorways and seem to have been hidden away to keep them safe. They may have been used by traders, instead of money, to buy goods.

These scales and weights date from around 2500 BCE and were used by Indus traders to weigh out goods.

Three Indus seals, dating from 2500–2000 BCE. The animal pictures were carved from soft stone and baked hard.

Weights and measures

Indus traders weighed out goods on copper scales, using weights, like the ones shown on the left. The weights are made from cubes of chert (a type of stone), and range from 0.8 grams to more than 10 kilograms. The same standard system of weights was used throughout the Indus Valley. Groups of weights have been found near the gateways of cities. They may have been used by officials when collecting taxes on goods entering the city.

Sealing the deal

Among the earliest Indus artefacts found were square or rectangular stone seals, about the size of postage stamps. They are carved with pictures of animals and symbols which look like writing (see page 22). When a seal was pressed into soft clay, it left an impression. The dried clay could then be used as a label or tag, and tied to a pot, basket or sack to show that it belonged to a particular trader or group of traders.

 ## Around the world

c. 3000 BCE Mesopotamia
Hoards of metal axes found in Mesopotamia may have been used by Mesopotamian traders in exchange for goods.

c. 3000–500 BCE Egypt
The Egyptians use a system of weights, called deben. These are used to calculate the value of goods by comparing them to their weight in silver or copper.

c. 1600–1460 BCE China
In the Shang Dynasty, cowrie shells are highly valued as money. Later, copies in bone, stone or bronze are used instead of natural shells.

GETTING ABOUT

Most Indus people did not travel far from home, but traders made long and difficult journeys, by land, river and sea. Some traders carried goods on their backs. Others used wooden carts, pulled by bullocks, like the carts still used in Pakistan and India today.

Carts pulled by bullocks are still used throughout India and Pakistan. Archaeologists at Indus Valley sites have found small clay models of similar carts.

Indus boats

Pictures on seals show the boats used by Indus traders. Some boats were small, with flat bottoms for travelling on rivers. One seal shows a boat with raised ends, a square cabin in the middle, and a rolled-up sail. It may have been used for longer journeys by sea. No sails have ever been found, but we know that the Indus people grew cotton and flax which could have been used to make sail cloth.

Trading evidence

We have plenty of evidence that Indus traders sailed to Arabia. Beads, axes, ivory combs and other artefacts have been discovered along the coast. There are also fragments of large black storage jars, used for carrying grain, and possibly as ballast for ships. Most importantly, slabs of bitumen (tar) have been found which may be the remains of Indus ships.

Lothal docks

Lothal is an ancient Indus port on the west coast of modern-day India. It was an important centre of the bead industry. From here, ships sailed to Arabia and Mesopotamia. Archaeologists have excavated a sunken, rectangular space, surrounded by a brick wall. Some experts think that it was a space where ships docked.

The remains of the ancient harbour at Lothal. Indus traders set out from here on long, risky journeys by ship.

Around the world

c. 3200 BCE Egypt
The Egyptians begin to use large, rectangular sails to push along their boats. This makes it much easier to sail up the River Nile, using the power of the wind.

c. 3200 BCE Mesopotamia
The Mesopotamians use square-rigged sailing boats to establish trade routes with places as far away as the Indus Valley. They also have river boats made from reeds and animal skins.

c. 1500 BCE Egypt
Queen Hatshepsut sends out a daring sea expedition to the Land of Punt, in modern-day Ethiopia. The ships bring back many goods, including live myrrh trees.

WORDS AND PICTURES

Experts believe that the Indus people had a system of picture writing. Examples have been found on seals, clay tablets, pottery and a signboard that may have hung over a gateway. Unfortunately, no one has yet been able to read what the writing says or find out what language the people spoke.

22

If we could decipher the writing on the Indus seals, we could find out a great deal more about how Indus people lived.

Picture writing

At least 400 different Indus picture signs have been identified. This is too many for them to be a single alphabet, but not enough for there to be a different sign for every word. Each inscription is very short, with only around five signs. Writing was probably done using a sharp stick or tool, and may have been linked to trade, religion or government.

Cutting edge

For centuries, people could not read the scripts of ancient Egypt and Sumeria. They were only able to read them when texts were discovered that had examples of both a known language and the ancient one. By comparing the two, they worked out what the ancient script said. For Egypt, this text was a stone slab, called the Rosetta Stone. It had the same piece of text in three different scripts.

23

Cracking the code

Since the 1900s, many experts have worked at deciphering Indus writing. At first, they compared it to Sumerian cuneiform (wedge-shaped) writing, which looked similar, but the two scripts were not related. Today, computers are being used to try to crack the code. So far, nothing has been successful. Some people think that the script may be similar to Tamil, a language spoken today in South India. Others think that the marks are not a form of writing at all.

By comparing the scripts on the Rosetta Stone, one of which was in Greek, experts were able to work out the meaning of ancient Egyptian hieroglyphs, or picture writing.

Around the world

c. 4000–3000 BCE Sumeria
Some of the earliest examples of writing are wedge-shaped cuneiform characters on clay tablets from Sumeria. The inscriptions are temple records.

c. 3200 BCE Egypt
The Egyptians become one of the first civilisations to invent a system of writing. It uses picture symbols, called hieroglyphs, to stand for sounds and objects.

c. 1200–1050 BCE China
The first evidence of Chinese writing comes from inscriptions on bones from the late Shang Dynasty. The bones are used to communicate with the spirits of the ancestors.

INDUS BELIEFS

Unlike the ancient Egyptians and Sumerians, the Indus people did not leave behind any temples, religious texts or statues of the gods. This makes it difficult to find out exactly what they believed. There are many different ideas, based on comparisons with other ancient civilisations, and looking at the evidence that we have.

Indus imagery

From pictures on seals and clay tablets, and from clay masks and small statues, experts think that the Indus people worshipped a number of gods and goddesses linked to nature. Female figures may have been fertility goddesses who, people believed, made their crops grow. Clay masks of people and animals may have been worn in religious ceremonies to act out myths and legends.

Some archaeologists think that figures like this one were goddesses, worshipped by the Indus people.

Indus influence

Some experts think that Indus beliefs shaped the Indian religions that came after them. This seal seems to show a male god with three faces and horns. He is surrounded by animals — an elephant, tiger, rhinoceros and water buffalo — and looks similar to Shiva, one of the most important Hindu gods. Other seals show the pipal (fig) tree which is a sacred tree in Hinduism and Buddhism.

Seal stories

Some Indus seals may have been used for telling stories. One seal shows a female figure, fighting off two tigers. She is accompanied by an elephant. On the other side of the seal, a man kills a water buffalo with a spear. Seals like this one may have been used to tell stories about the lives and adventures of the gods and goddesses.

The Pashupati Seal found at Mohenjo-Daro dates from c. 2500–2400 BCE. It can now be seen in the National Museum, New Delhi, India.

25

Around the world

c. 2100 BCE Sumeria
The Sumerian king, Ur-Nammu, builds a great ziggurat (stepped temple) to the Moon god at Ur. It is 64 metres long and over 30 metres high.

1364–1347 BCE Egypt
Reign of Akhenaten, previously known as Amenhotep IV. He bans the worship of the old Egyptian gods and goddesses and introduces the worship of one god, Aten.

900 BCE India
Religious poems composed by Aryan priests are gathered together to form a collection, called the *Rig Veda*. It remains one of the most sacred texts of the Hindu religion.

DEATH AND BURIAL

It seems that the people of the Indus Valley Civilisation may have believed in a life after death. Many graves have been found which shows that people took care in how they buried their dead. Buried alongside the dead were many personal belongings, perhaps acting as offerings to the gods and goddesses or for use in the next world.

26

A skeleton from the Indus Valley Civilisation shows that people were buried carefully when they died.

Health
From burials, archaeologists estimate that Indus people lived to around 31 years of age. Some people showed signs of arthritis in their spines, possibly as a result of carrying heavy loads on their heads. In general, though, people seemed to have had good health, probably because of their varied diet.

Burial places

Large cemeteries at Harappa and Kalibangan show that the Indus people set aside special places for burying their dead. In one of the cemeteries at Harappa, some bodies were buried in brick-lined pits and others in wooden coffins, with their heads pointing north and their feet pointing south. In the other cemetery at Harappa, some bodies are buried in pots.

Grave goods

Across the ancient world, dead people were buried with their belongings, which were known as grave goods. The main goods buried with Indus people were pots – up to 40 have been found in one grave – goblets and plates. They may have been used for a feast at the person's funeral, then placed in the grave. Archaeologists have also found beads, copper mirrors, stone tools and the remains of sheep and goats.

27

This large clay pot may have been used to bury a body. Many pots were also placed in graves.

Around the world

c. 5000–3000 BCE South America

The oldest mummies known come from the Chinchorro culture in northern Chile and southern Peru. Around 280 have been found, of men, women and children.

c. 2600 BCE Egypt

The Egyptians use mummification to preserve bodies so that their souls can travel into the afterlife. Their techniques worked so well that many mummies have survived to this day.

1600–1460 BCE China

Many bronze pots, jars and cups have been found in royal Shang tombs. They are buried with their owners for making offerings of food and drink to ancestors in the afterlife.

END OF THE INDUS

From around 1900 BCE, the great Indus Valley Civilisation started to fall apart. At its peak, it had lasted for less than a thousand years. Life in the cities began to break down, and by 1700 BCE, most of them had been abandoned and gradually fell into ruins. Experts are still not sure about what caused the decline, but there are many different theories.

28

Invasion theory

In the 1940s, British archaeologist Mortimer Wheeler discovered a group of human skeletons – men, women and children – among the ruins of Mohenjo-Daro. He believed that they had been killed by invaders who had conquered the Indus cities. Today, archaeologists do not think that this is true. There were no signs that the cities had been attacked or of the Indus people fighting back. They seemed to have been peace-loving – very few Indus weapons have been found.

Were these people killed by attackers who went on to destroy the Indus Valley Civilisation?

Natural disaster

Other experts believe that a natural disaster may have been to blame. The Indus climate grew cooler and drier, and the monsoon rains failed (see box). Alternatively, the river, or its tributaries, may have changed course, causing floods in some places and drought in others. All of these events would have caused food crops to fail, leading to famine and disease.

Some experts think that damage caused by an earthquake may have led to the city of Dholavira, shown here, being abandoned.

29

Cutting edge
The latest thinking by experts is that a long-term drought caused the Indus Valley Civilisation to collapse. Based on information from an ancient lake in India, they believe that the regular summer monsoon rains, which were vital for farming, stopped for around 200 years. This caused a series of droughts from which the Indus Valley Civilisation never recovered.

Around the world

c. 2371 BCE Sumeria
King Sargon of Akkad conquers Sumeria and makes it part of his growing empire. His empire falls apart after his death in 2316 BCE.

c. 1046 BCE China
At the Battle of Muye, the Shang king, Di Xin, is defeated by Wu of Zhou, bringing an end to the Shang and marking the start of the Zhou Dynasty.

30 BCE Egypt
Egypt becomes part of the Roman Empire after the death of Queen Cleopatra, the last of the Ptolemies, the family that ruled Egypt from 323 BCE.

GLOSSARY

Archaeologists People who study human history by excavating ancient ruins and remains, such as cities, tombs and artefacts.

Artefact An object, such as jewellery or a statue, that was made long ago.

Arthritis An illness in which the sufferer has painful or stiff joints.

Cesspits Pits dug to dispose of waste, such as sewage.

Citadel A building in a city which may have been used as a hiding place if the city came under attack.

Cuneiform The system of writing used in ancient Mesopotamia. It used wedge-shaped letters.

Drought A long period of dry weather combined with very little or no rain.

Faience Type of glazed clay or earthenware, made by heating powdered quartz (a mineral).

Fermented The process by which grain and grapes are turned into beer and wine.

Fertile Land with rich soil which is good for growing crops.

Hieroglyphs Pictures or signs used as writing in ancient Egypt.

Inscription Words that are carved or engraved on a coin, wall or statue.

Irrigation System of canals, ditches and pipes used by farmers to bring water to their fields so that their crops can grow.

Kilns Oven-like structures where potters fire (harden) their pots.

Monsoon A regular system of winds that brings rain to parts of Asia.

Reservoir A large tank or man-made lake, used for storing water.

Sanitation A system used for getting rid of waste water and sewage from people's homes.

Sewage Waste from people's homes that is carried away in drains.

Tributaries Streams or small rivers that feed into larger rivers.

30

WEBSITES

http://www.bbc.co.uk/schools/primaryhistory/indus_valley
Find out more about the Indus Valley
Civilisation on the BBC website and take a quiz
to find out how much you know about the Indus
way of life.

http://www.harappa.com/indus/slideindex.html
A set of 90 photographs which take you on a
tour of the ancient Indus cities of Harappa and
Mohenjo-Daro.

http://www.ancientindia.co.uk/indus/home_set.html
Read the story of an Indus bead-maker's son,
then explore Mohenjo-Daro and find out more
about how it was excavated.

Note to parents and teachers
Every effort has been made by the Publishers to ensure
that the web sites in this book are suitable for children,
that they are of the highest educational value, and that they
contain no inappropriate or offensive material. However,
because of the nature of the Internet, it is impossible
to guarantee that the contents of these sites will not be
altered. We strongly advise that Internet access is supervised
by a responsible adult.

TIMELINE

c. 3000 BCE Small farming communities are
established in the Indus Valley in north-west India
(now Pakistan).

c. 2600 BCE These early settlements develop into
cities. Indus script is used.

c. 2600–1900 BCE The Indus Valley Civilisation
reaches the peak of its powers.

c. 2500–2400 BCE The Great Bath is built at
Mohenjo-Daro.

c. 2400 BCE Written texts from Mesopotamia
talk about Meluhha which may have been the
Indus Valley.

c. 1900–1700 BCE The Indus Valley Civilisation
begins to decline. Cities are abandoned and fall
into ruin.

1826 CE British traveller Charles Masson discovers
a group of brick mounds which are the ruins of the
Indus city of Harappa.

1872 CE British archaeologist, Alexander
Cunningham, finds the first Indus seal. Since
then, thousands more have been found.

1920s CE Archaeologists being to excavate the
ruins of Harappa and Mohenjo-Daro.

1927 CE The 'Priest-King' statue is found in
Mohenjo-Daro.

INDEX

32